Adventures in Art

Marc Chagall

Life is a Dream

Prestel

The Village and I

is the title given to this picture by the painter Marc Chagall, and in it he painted a large profile of his own head.

The village is called Vitebsk and is really a small town in Russia with two rivers, bridges, churches, palaces and many wooden houses.
Marc Chagall was born there on 7th July 1887.
The gardens in front of the houses were full of flowers, vegetables and herbs, and in the little farmyards and outbuildings there lived cows, pigs, horses, donkeys and chickens. The artist spent his childhood in a large family amongst all these animals, which are to be found again and again in his pictures.

The animals were his friends, and he often used to talk to them. What do you think he is saying here to the white cow? Or is the cow telling him a story?

The picture *The Village and I* tells many stories and is made up of different shapes and colours — like a

Kaleidoscope, Kaleidoscope,

in which new a pattern appears each time you turn it: small, brightly-coloured wooden houses, two of which are upside-down, a man looking out of the church with its round dome, a farmer walking across the field with a scythe, the farmer's wife showing him the way — but wait: she is upside-down too! And the white cow appears twice in the picture.

A picture of Vitebsk emerges from the many individual elements of this painting, although it is difficult to know whether Chagall is depicting a dream or drawing on actual memories. It is not easy to tell them apart, because Chagall's head was always filled with images of his village — of the houses, the people and the animals — no matter where he happened to be living at the time.

The Fiddler

Throughout the year celebrations were held in
the little Russian town — and there were always
fiddlers there to play music.

Marc Chagall loved the musicians, the cheerful sounds of their waltzes and polkas

But they could also play quiet, sad songs.

Since one of these musicians lived with Chagall's family,
he was allowed to play the violin from time to time when
he was a little boy.

What do you think the fiddler with the green
face is playing?
He stands like a giant in the snowy landscape,
towering above the village. A group of three
brightly-dressed figures looks up at him in
amazement. As he plays, the violin magically
turns yellow and, in the middle of winter, a
blue fairy-tale tree begins to bloom at his feet.

The Birthday

Marc Chagall lived in a little house by the river, where he was able to paint in peace. Bella, his fiancée, often visited him there. She always brought flowers with her, because Chagall was so fond of them.

On Chagall's birthday, Bella could hardly wait to celebrate it with him. She walked through fields and climbed over fences to pick a whole armful of flowers. At home she donned her most beautiful dress and packed a freshly-baked cake to take with her. Then she ran through the town to the little house by the river.

Bella was just about to give Chagall the colourful bouquet of flowers when he shouted, 'Don't move!' and proceeded to assemble his paintbrushes and to squeeze the paints out of the tubes onto his palette:

red

white

blue

black

green

On the wall there are brightly-coloured tapestries. Bella's dress is swirling round her legs. Suddenly Chagall lifted Bella off the floor and it seemed to her as if they were floating up to the ceiling together. They were very happy and in love!

6

Bouquet of Flowers

Chagall enjoyed painting flowers. They appear time and again in his pictures as small individual flowers or as large bouquets.

The flowers here bloom in red, yellow, white, orange and pink, and glow like stars in the night. The air is cool and blue. The leaves and blossoms rise up into the sky. Do you think the flower-fairy used her magic to make the bouquet grow so large?

Chagall spent much of his time in the countryside — not only in Vitebsk, but also later in France. There, he painted the blue of the sky, the light of the sun and the bright colours of the flowers.

Self-Portrait with Seven Fingers

All dressed up, with a yellow waistcoat, a spotted shirt and a necktie, Marc Chagall sits in front of his easel. He has even put a rose in his buttonhole. In his right hand he is holding some paintbrushes and a palette covered with various paints — red, green, yellow, violet.

He has big eyes. He would like to look at everything very closely, so that he can paint it. It is as though he is saying with this self-portrait: "I am a painter, and *what* a painter at that!"

Chagall moved from Russia to Paris. Many famous artists lived in the French capital at that time. He hoped to learn from them and eventually become a great painter himself.

Chagall was fascinated by the great city of Paris: the Eiffel Tower, the crowds of people, the cars, the numerous museums and the pictures by other painters. His head was also still filled with memories of Vitebsk, its many animals and wooden houses.

One hand was not enough to paint all this — he would need at least seven fingers!

Nor was there enough canvas to paint so many pictures. Since Chagall had very little money, he took tablecloths, sheets and even his nightshirt, cut them up into pieces and painted on them instead.

All day and all night he painted pictures of Paris, Vitebsk and all his dreams and fantasies.

The Eiffel Tower

The Eiffel Tower was tired of standing all alone, stretching high above Paris, where he could see Paris only from afar. He thought to himself: 'There must surely be much more to discover in this city!'

So he put on a cap and some shoes, and set off with a pipe in his mouth. As he was wondering where to go on his journey, a colourful donkey came along. There were bells hanging around its neck which jingled cheerfully when it walked. It also had a travelling companion: a cockerel, which can be seen wandering or flying through many of Chagall's other pictures. It did not take the Eiffel Tower long to make up his mind and set off with the two of them. Together, they wandered merrily through the blue, grey and green.

Where do you think they went?

Or, did the Eiffel Tower not really move at all? Isn't it still there, standing all alone, high above the city?

Was it all just a dream?

Paris through the Window

What is on the outside and what is on the inside in this picture?
The city of Paris, with the Eiffel Tower clearly recognizable, is
separated from the inside of a room by a colourful lattice
window. Perhaps we are looking out of Chagall's studio.
The outside world, the world that Chagall saw every day, was
mixed up with his inner world, with his fantasies and dreams.

Here,
a cat has a
human face, a train
is travelling upside-down,
people going for a walk float
through the city, while a man,
who hangs from a triangle,
is gliding through
the colourful
sky above
Paris.

Is this why the man in the
foreground has two faces?
A blue, mysterious one, with
which he looks inward at his
dreams and fantasies, and a
light-coloured, cheerful one
that closely observes the
world around him?

14

The Dance

Marc Chagall looked at the world in a different
way from most people. A new world grew out of
his imagination, a world in which people and
things leave their usual places, float around and
stand on their heads.

The big, round sun shines brightly and bathes everything in a
cheerful yellow.
Whatever is this strange red creature playing the violin?
The sounds of the music draw lines that whirl about in the
yellow atmosphere, while the lovers sway to the music.
A green woman holding a bouquet is attracted by the melody
and floats towards the violin player.
Chagall has also painted himself in this picture: he can be seen
with a palette in hand, sliding down a sunbeam with a violet-
coloured cockerel.

"Now your colours are singing", said a friend
of Chagall's about pictures such as this one.

Everything in this painting seems to float and is full of music

The Lovers

In winter white snowflakes dance through the
air, in spring pink, violet and blue blossoms,
in summer yellow sunbeams, and in autumn
red, orange and green leaves.

The Colours mingle, glow and whirl through the picture

The moon quietly slips down lower and lower to
hide amongst the coloured dots — he is happy
to be just a guest at this festival of colour, and not
to have to light it himself!
Everybody seems contented: the lovers are
embracing each other and a clown is picking
flowers — or is he picking colours?

Blue Circus

Marc Chagall loved going to the circus, especially with his daughter, Ida. They were therefore very lucky that a good friend of theirs rented a private box in a circus, which enabled them to go there every day. Many things that Chagall saw at the circus were depicted later in his paintings.

Like his pictures, the circus is a colourful world full of mysterious figures, tightrope walkers, magicians, clowns, acrobats, musicians and dancers. In this magical world everything seems to be possible! What is a dream, what is reality in the big top? And in Chagall's pictures?

Here, the circus princess is swinging from the trapeze in a beam of light shining through the deep blue

The cockerel on her leg is beating time on a drum. The shining moon has grown a fin so that it can hold the violin better. A green horse and a flying fish are admiring the trapeze artist, who is even being presented with flowers!

20

The Juggler

What kind of creature can this juggler
possibly be?
A human being, an animal or an angel?
And what is he dancing on?
He seems to be standing firmly on the earth,
as roots and branches are growing up his leg.
And yet, it looks as though he is just about to
take off with his big, white wings.

The rainbow is a guest in this strange circus; a trapeze artist
is suspended above its brightly-coloured rays. The horse rider is
making her entrance on the roof of a farmhouse, while a colourful
horse is growing out of the rainbow and is looking at her

There are spectators at this performance, too.
Some of them are sitting around the circus arena,
others on the rainbow.

This is not a real circus tent; instead,
it seems as though the whole world
has suddenly become a circus!

The Flying Sleigh

The houses were asleep and the village lay under a blanket of snow.
Suddenly the sleigh went faster and faster over the hard, frozen
ground and up over the rooftops, flying through the cold, dark-blue
winter night. There was a rushing and roaring sound as they flew
through the air. The small, thin moon was now far below them.

They had still not reached their destination when the
farmer in the sleigh asked the brightly-coloured cockerel with
horses' hooves to slow down. It was icy cold and he had just seen
a large, silver samovar for making hot tea perched on a rooftop.
His glowing-red wife with the child in her arms also fancied
a cup of tea as they flew past.

The houses continue to sleep;
the moon sinks lower and lower,
until finally resting on a rooftop.
High above, a blue man waves
them onward.

Where do you think this
journey will take them next?

24

The Magician

This picture is completely bathed in blue. But
hidden in the blue are churches, houses and part of
the Eiffel Tower. Once again, Chagall has painted
Paris. We have also seen the lovers and the flowers
before in other pictures.

But who is

this strange,

colourful

figure?

He is holding something like a palette in his hand; his
whole body is made up of patches and patterns of colour.
The painter is the magician who takes the world as we see
it, and colours and transforms it in pictures.

It is
the artist's
job to search out
and portray things that
are hidden from most
people. If we let ourselves
be enchanted by him, we can
discover a whole new world!
Things can leave their usual
places, change colours, stand
on their heads and tell stories!

Marc Chagall's Life

Marc Chagall was born on 7th July 1887 in Vitebsk, Russia. He had seven sisters and two brothers. His father worked for a fishmonger and his mother kept a small shop. Their hospitable house was always full of visitors.

After attending elementary school, Chagall moved to St Petersburg to study under Leon Bakst at the Zvantseva School of Art. From 1910 to 1914, he lived in Paris, where he had a studio in the Impasse du Maine and met many painters and writers.

On 25th July 1915, in Vitebsk, he married Bella Rosenfeld, whom he never tired of painting. In 1916, their daughter Ida was born and, three years later, Chagall founded an art school in Vitebsk. The Chagalls moved to Paris in 1923, but spent much of their time in the French countryside. From 1941 to 1946, they lived in America, where Bella died in 1944.

After returning to Paris, Chagall had many exhibitions and travelled extensively. In 1950, he moved to the south of France and, two years later, married Valentine (Vava) Brodsky, who enabled him to carry on painting in peace into his old age. Besides painting, he also designed stained-glass windows and stage scenery. On 28th March 1985, Marc Chagall died at the age of ninety-seven in Saint-Paul-de-Vence near Nice.